Diary

of

a

Meanderer

AF449678

Copyright © 2019 A.Verma

All rights reserved.

The views and opinions expressed in this journal are those of the author and are meant for general information purposes only. The information provided in this journal is intended only as a guide and readers are advised to verify before acting on the basis of any information.

Contents

1.Personal Information

2.Trip 1

•Planning checklists

•Preparation checklists

•Packing checklists

•Travel Details at a glance

•Travel Itinerary

•Travel Budget at a glance

•Memory Lane

3. Trip 2

•Planning checklists

•Preparation checklists

•Packing checklists

•Travel Details at a glance

•Travel Itinerary

•Travel Budget at a glance

•Memory Lane

4. Trip 3

•Planning checklists

•Preparation checklists

•Packing checklists

•Travel Details at a glance

•Travel Itinerary

•Travel Budget at a glance

•Memory Lane

Contents

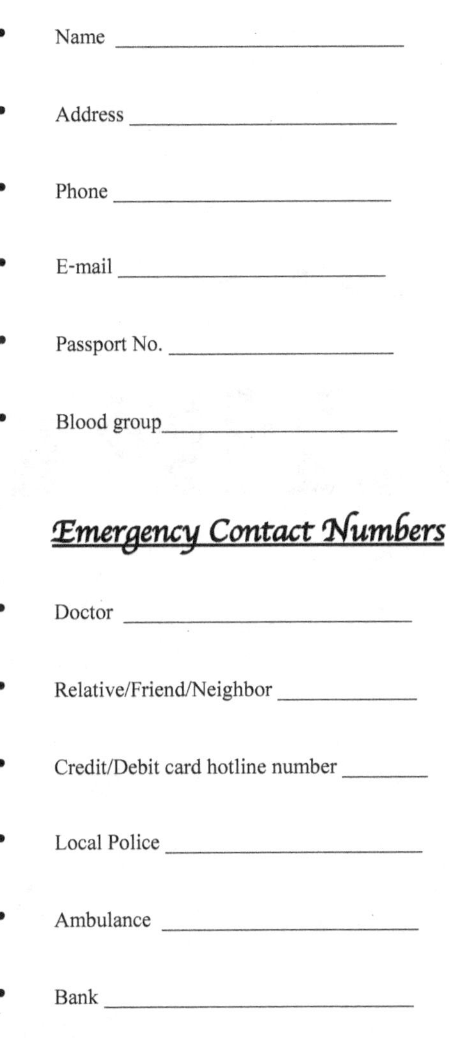

<u>*Personal Information*</u>

- Name _______________________

- Address _______________________

- Phone _______________________

- E-mail _______________________

- Passport No. _______________________

- Blood group_______________________

<u>*Emergency Contact Numbers*</u>

- Doctor _______________________

- Relative/Friend/Neighbor _______________________

- Credit/Debit card hotline number _______________________

- Local Police _______________________

- Ambulance _______________________

- Bank _______________________

- Insurance _______________________

TRIP 1:

PLANNING

- ☐ Check out a few famous travel websites for things to see, do, and other basic information regarding your destination.
- ☐ Search for the best time to visit, based on weather (check weather at AccuWeather.com)
- ☐ Look for special holiday packages
- ☐ Watch YouTube videos
- ☐ Read travel guidebooks
- ☐ Make a list of places to visit, note their hours of opening, closing and the entrance fees
- ☐ Apply for visa (if applicable)
- ☐ Book flights
- ☐ Take insurance (travel/ medical)
- ☐ Book accommodation
- ☐ Book internal transportation
- ☐ Get vaccinations
- ☐ If traveling internationally, convert your money to local currency (of destination)

- ☐ Activate international roaming or get an international sim card
- ☐ Prepare a day-to-day itinerary
- ☐ Make a list of all the places, restaurants that you want to visit
- ☐ Make a list of all the activities that you plan to do
- ☐ Prepare a list of stores /restaurants near your apartment (in case you are renting an apartment)
- ☐ Note important numbers such as ambulance, local police
- ☐ _______________
- ☐ _______________
- ☐ _______________
- ☐ _______________
- ☐ _______________
- ☐ _______________
- ☐ _______________
- ☐ _______________
- ☐ _______________
- ☐ _______________
- ☐ _______________
- ☐ _______________

PLANNING

PLACES TO SEE

RESTAURANTS/ CAFES TO VISIT

PLANNING

ACTIVITIES TO DO	NOTES

PREPARATION

Essential Foreign Language Vocabulary

Word/Phrase in Foreign Language	Word/Phrase in English

Essential Foreign Language Vocabulary

Word/Phrase in Foreign Language	Word/Phrase in English

PREPARATION

THINGS TO DO

THINGS TO BUY

PREPARATION

THINGS TO DO ONE WEEK BEFORE...

- ☐ Personal grooming : skin/ nail/ hair care
- ☐ Go for a health check up
- ☐ Visit dentist
- ☐ Download a few travel apps
- ☐ Clean house
- ☐ Put valuables in a safe place
- ☐ Take care of your plants
- ☐ Take care of your pet
- ☐ Pay bills
- ☐ Buy medicines and other essentials
- ☐ Make copies of important travel documents
- ☐ Mail all important documents to yourself
- ☐ Buy and stock up on non-perishable food items
- ☐ Clean the refrigerator and get rid of perishables
- ☐ Web check-in (if available)
- ☐ Get car serviced (if traveling by car)
- ☐ Leave your itinerary with someone

- ☐ Confirm all your reservations
- ☐ Get packing done !
- ☐ _______________
- ☐ _______________
- ☐ _______________
- ☐ _______________
- ☐ _______________
- ☐ _______________
- ☐ _______________
- ☐ _______________
- ☐ _______________
- ☐ _______________
- ☐ _______________
- ☐ _______________
- ☐ _______________
- ☐ _______________
- ☐ _______________
- ☐ _______________
- ☐ _______________
- ☐ _______________
- ☐ _______________
- ☐ _______________
- ☐ _______________
- ☐ _______________
- ☐ _______________
- ☐ _______________
- ☐ _______________

PREPARATION

THINGS TO DO ONE DAY BEFORE...

- ☐ Charge all your electronic devices
- ☐ Switch off digital clocks
- ☐ Turn off appliances
- ☐ Turn off heating/cooling
- ☐ Turn off water
- ☐ Empty trash
- ☐ Hold newspapers
- ☐ Inform milkman
- ☐ Inform friends/neighbors
- ☐ Book a taxi for airport
- ☐ Weigh luggage
- ☐ Lock all windows, doors
- ☐ Cover all surfaces, devices, equipment
- ☐ Have a light homemade meal
- ☐ Sleep early to wake up fresh and all ready for your trip! :)
- ☐ _______________
- ☐ _______________
- ☐ _______________
- ☐ _______________
- ☐ _______________
- ☐ _______________
- ☐ _______________
- ☐ _______________

PACKING

CLOTHING & SHOES

- ☐ T-shirts
- ☐ Shirts
- ☐ Dresses
- ☐ Underwear
- ☐ Jeans/Pants
- ☐ Shorts
- ☐ Sweater
- ☐ Jacket
- ☐ Pajamas/ Sleepwear
- ☐ Swimsuit/ Swim Trunk
- ☐ Socks
- ☐ Stockings
- ☐ Skirts
- ☐ Raincoat
- ☐ Overcoat
- ☐ Joggers/Sweatpants
- ☐ Thermal Wear
- ☐ Walking Shoes
- ☐ Runners
- ☐ Flip Flops/ Slippers
- ☐ Heels
- ☐ Sandals
- ☐ Boots
- ☐ Shoe Bag
- ☐ Shoe Horn
- ☐ __________
- ☐ __________

ACCESSORIES

- ☐ Glasses
- ☐ Ties
- ☐ Scarves
- ☐ Earrings
- ☐ Jewelry
- ☐ Hats
- ☐ Caps
- ☐ Shawls/Wraps
- ☐ Belts
- ☐ Money Belt
- ☐ Beachwear
- ☐ Sunglasses
- ☐ Glasses Case
- ☐ Gloves
- ☐ Towels
- ☐ Handkerchiefs
- ☐ Swimming Gear
- ☐ Hair Accessories
- ☐ __________
- ☐ __________
- ☐ __________
- ☐ __________
- ☐ __________
- ☐ __________
- ☐ __________
- ☐ __________
- ☐ __________

PACKING

MEDICATION

- ☐ First aid kit
- ☐ Prescribed medicine
- ☐ Prescription copy
- ☐ Allergy medicine
- ☐ Pain killers
- ☐ Motion sickness pills
- ☐ Altitude sickness pills
- ☐ Insect repellant
- ☐ Common cold
- ☐ Vitamins
- ☐ Antibiotics
- ☐ Contraception
- ☐ Laxatives
- ☐ Diarrhea medicine
- ☐ Eye drops
- ☐ Sleeping pills
- ☐ Sickness bags
- ☐ _______________
- ☐ _______________
- ☐ _______________
- ☐ _______________
- ☐ _______________
- ☐ _______________
- ☐ _______________
- ☐ _______________
- ☐ _______________
- ☐ _______________

ELECTRONICS / TECH GEAR

- ☐ Phone
- ☐ Phone charger
- ☐ Laptop
- ☐ Laptop charger
- ☐ Watch
- ☐ Headphones
- ☐ Travel alarm clock
- ☐ Hair dryer
- ☐ E-reader
- ☐ E-reader charger
- ☐ iPad
- ☐ iPod
- ☐ Electric shaver
- ☐ Extra batteries
- ☐ Adapters
- ☐ Power banks
- ☐ Camera
- ☐ Camera charger
- ☐ Memory cards
- ☐ Selfie stick
- ☐ Tripod
- ☐ Travel iron
- ☐ Portable hotspot
- ☐ Portable luggage weighing scale
- ☐ _______________
- ☐ _______________
- ☐ _______________

PACKING

TOILETRIES

- [ ] Toothbrush
- [ ] Toothpaste
- [ ] Dental floss
- [ ] Mouth wash
- [ ] Hair brush
- [ ] Razors
- [ ] Soap
- [ ] Shampoo
- [ ] Conditioner
- [ ] Deodorant
- [ ] Perfume
- [ ] Nail clipper
- [ ] Nail filer
- [ ] Tweezers
- [ ] Ear buds
- [ ] Hand sanitizer
- [ ] Pocket tissues
- [ ] Toiletry kit
- [ ] Contact lens kit
- [ ] Face wash
- [ ] Toner
- [ ] Feminine hygiene products
- [ ] Moisturizer
- [ ] Sunblock
- [ ] Night creams
- [ ] Make up
- [ ] Talcum
- [ ] Oil

TOILETRIES

- [ ] Lip balm
- [ ] Lipsticks, lip gloss
- [ ] Hand cream
- [ ] Make up kit
- [ ] Make up remover
- [ ] Wipe pads
- [ ] Nail polish
- [ ] Nail polish remover
- [ ] Cotton pads
- [ ] Small travel mirror
- [ ] Toilet paper
- [ ] Small scissors
- [ ] Laundry detergent
- [ ] Shaving kit
- [ ] __________
- [ ] __________
- [ ] __________
- [ ] __________
- [ ] __________
- [ ] __________
- [ ] __________
- [ ] __________
- [ ] __________
- [ ] __________
- [ ] __________
- [ ] __________
- [ ] __________
- [ ] __________

PACKING

MONEY & DOCUMENTS

- ☐ Cash (local and foreign currency)
- ☐ Few US dollars
- ☐ Forex cards
- ☐ Credit cards
- ☐ Debit cards
- ☐ Travelers checks
- ☐ Emergency money
- ☐ Passport
- ☐ Visa
- ☐ Airline tickets
- ☐ Identification cards
- ☐ Boarding pass
- ☐ Copies of documents
- ☐ Driving license
- ☐ Hotel reservation document
- ☐ Insurance cards
- ☐ Passport size photos
- ☐ Travel itinerary
- ☐ _______________
- ☐ _______________
- ☐ _______________
- ☐ _______________
- ☐ _______________
- ☐ _______________
- ☐ _______________

MISCELLANEOUS

- ☐ Wallet
- ☐ Safety pins
- ☐ Keys
- ☐ Sewing kit
- ☐ Ziplock bags
- ☐ Laundry bag
- ☐ Backpack
- ☐ Handbag
- ☐ Purse
- ☐ Beach bag
- ☐ Snacks
- ☐ Sleeping mask
- ☐ Eye mask
- ☐ Ear plugs
- ☐ Travel pillow
- ☐ Personal diary/journal
- ☐ Pen
- ☐ Umbrella
- ☐ Water bottle
- ☐ Cards/other games
- ☐ Travel/language guide
- ☐ Maps
- ☐ Travel flashlight
- ☐ Tea/coffee sachets
- ☐ Duct tape
- ☐ An extra bag
- ☐ Yoga mat
- ☐ _______________

PACKING

MISCELLANEOUS

MISCELLANEOUS

TRAVEL DETAILS AT A GLANCE

FLIGHT DETAILS

NAME OF DESTINATION			
DATE OF DEPARTURE			
NAME OF AIRPORT			
FLIGHT NUMBER			
TIME OF DEPARTURE			
TIME OF ARRIVAL			

ACCOMMODATION

NAME OF HOTEL/ OTHER			
LOCATION OF LODGING			
CHECK-IN TIME			
CHECK-OUT TIME			
ROOM NUMBER			

TRAVEL ITINERARY

Day	Things to do
1	
2	
3	
4	
5	
6	
7	
8	
9	
10	

TRAVEL ITINERARY

Day	Things to do
11	
12	
13	
14	
15	
16	
17	
18	
19	
20	

TRAVEL BUDGET AT A GLANCE

EXPENSES FOR	ESTIMATED	ACTUAL
TRANSPORTATION		
FLIGHTS		
TAXI/TRAIN/ BUS		
OTHER		
TOTAL		
ACCOMMODATION		
HOTEL/APARTMENT		
OTHER		
TOTAL		
MEALS		
BREAKFAST		
LUNCH		
TEA		
DINNER		
OTHER		
TOTAL		
DIVERTISSEMENTS		
SIGHTSEEING		
ACTIVITIES		
OTHER		
TOTAL		

TRAVEL BUDGET AT A GLANCE

EXPENSES FOR	ESTIMATED	ACTUAL
MISCELLANEOUS		
VISAS		
INSURANCE		
TRAVEL ESSENTIALS		
TOTAL		
TOTAL EXPENSES :		

MEMORY LANE...
Here you can write about some of your special
moments during this trip, put your photos...

TRIP 2:

PLANNING

- ❑ Check out a few famous travel websites for things to see, do, and other basic information regarding your destination.
- ❑ Search for the best time to visit, based on weather (check weather at AccuWeather.com)
- ❑ Look for special holiday packages
- ❑ Watch YouTube videos
- ❑ Read travel guidebooks
- ❑ Make a list of places to visit, note their hours of opening, closing and the entrance fees
- ❑ Apply for visa (if applicable)
- ❑ Book flights
- ❑ Take insurance (travel/ medical)
- ❑ Book accommodation
- ❑ Book internal transportation
- ❑ Get vaccinations
- ❑ If traveling internationally, convert your money to local currency (of destination)

- ❑ Activate international roaming or get an international sim card
- ❑ Prepare a day-to-day itinerary
- ❑ Make a list of all the places, restaurants that you want to visit
- ❑ Make a list of all the activities that you plan to do
- ❑ Prepare a list of stores /restaurants near your apartment (in case you are renting an apartment)
- ❑ Note important numbers such as ambulance, local police
- ❑ _______________
- ❑ _______________
- ❑ _______________
- ❑ _______________
- ❑ _______________
- ❑ _______________
- ❑ _______________
- ❑ _______________
- ❑ _______________
- ❑ _______________
- ❑ _______________
- ❑ _______________

PLANNING

PLACES TO SEE

- ☐ __________________
- ☐ __________________
- ☐ __________________
- ☐ __________________
- ☐ __________________
- ☐ __________________
- ☐ __________________
- ☐ __________________
- ☐ __________________
- ☐ __________________
- ☐ __________________
- ☐ __________________
- ☐ __________________
- ☐ __________________
- ☐ __________________
- ☐ __________________
- ☐ __________________
- ☐ __________________
- ☐ __________________
- ☐ __________________
- ☐ __________________
- ☐ __________________

RESTAURANT'S/ CAFES TO VISIT

- ☐ __________________
- ☐ __________________
- ☐ __________________
- ☐ __________________
- ☐ __________________
- ☐ __________________
- ☐ __________________
- ☐ __________________
- ☐ __________________
- ☐ __________________
- ☐ __________________
- ☐ __________________
- ☐ __________________
- ☐ __________________
- ☐ __________________
- ☐ __________________
- ☐ __________________
- ☐ __________________
- ☐ __________________
- ☐ __________________
- ☐ __________________
- ☐ __________________

PLANNING

ACTIVITIES TO DO

NOTES

PREPARATION

Essential Foreign Language Vocabulary

Word/Phrase in Foreign Language	Word/Phrase in English

PREPARATION

Essential Foreign Language Vocabulary

Word/Phrase in Foreign Language	Word/Phrase in English

PREPARATION

THINGS TO DO

THINGS TO BUY

PREPARATION

THINGS TO DO ONE WEEK BEFORE...

- ❏ Personal grooming : skin/ nail/ hair care
- ❏ Go for a health check up
- ❏ Visit dentist
- ❏ Download a few travel apps
- ❏ Clean house
- ❏ Put valuables in a safe place
- ❏ Take care of your plants
- ❏ Take care of your pet
- ❏ Pay bills
- ❏ Buy medicines and other essentials
- ❏ Make copies of important travel documents
- ❏ Mail all important documents to yourself
- ❏ Buy and stock up on non-perishable food items
- ❏ Clean the refrigerator and get rid of perishables
- ❏ Web check-in (if available)
- ❏ Get car serviced (if traveling by car)
- ❏ Leave your itinerary with someone

- ❏ Confirm all your reservations
- ❏ Get packing done !
- ❏ _______________
- ❏ _______________
- ❏ _______________
- ❏ _______________
- ❏ _______________
- ❏ _______________
- ❏ _______________
- ❏ _______________
- ❏ _______________
- ❏ _______________
- ❏ _______________
- ❏ _______________
- ❏ _______________
- ❏ _______________
- ❏ _______________
- ❏ _______________
- ❏ _______________
- ❏ _______________
- ❏ _______________
- ❏ _______________
- ❏ _______________
- ❏ _______________
- ❏ _______________
- ❏ _______________

PREPARATION

THINGS TO DO ONE DAY BEFORE...

- ☐ Charge all your electronic devices
- ☐ Switch off digital clocks
- ☐ Turn off appliances
- ☐ Turn off heating/cooling
- ☐ Turn off water
- ☐ Empty trash
- ☐ Hold newspapers
- ☐ Inform milkman
- ☐ Inform friends/neighbors
- ☐ Book a taxi for airport
- ☐ Weigh luggage
- ☐ Lock all windows, doors
- ☐ Cover all surfaces, devices, equipment
- ☐ Have a light homemade meal
- ☐ Sleep early to wake up fresh and all ready for your trip! :)
- ☐ _______________
- ☐ _______________
- ☐ _______________
- ☐ _______________
- ☐ _______________
- ☐ _______________
- ☐ _______________
- ☐ _______________

PACKING

CLOTHING & SHOES

- ☐ T-shirts
- ☐ Shirts
- ☐ Dresses
- ☐ Underwear
- ☐ Jeans/Pants
- ☐ Shorts
- ☐ Sweater
- ☐ Jacket
- ☐ Pajamas/ Sleepwear
- ☐ Swimsuit/ Swim Trunk
- ☐ Socks
- ☐ Stockings
- ☐ Skirts
- ☐ Raincoat
- ☐ Overcoat
- ☐ Joggers/Sweatpants
- ☐ Thermal Wear
- ☐ Walking Shoes
- ☐ Runners
- ☐ Flip Flops/ Slippers
- ☐ Heels
- ☐ Sandals
- ☐ Boots
- ☐ Shoe Bag
- ☐ Shoe Horn
- ☐ __________
- ☐ __________

ACCESSORIES

- ☐ Glasses
- ☐ Ties
- ☐ Scarves
- ☐ Earrings
- ☐ Jewelry
- ☐ Hats
- ☐ Caps
- ☐ Shawls/Wraps
- ☐ Belts
- ☐ Money Belt
- ☐ Beachwear
- ☐ Sunglasses
- ☐ Glasses Case
- ☐ Gloves
- ☐ Towels
- ☐ Handkerchiefs
- ☐ Swimming Gear
- ☐ Hair Accessories
- ☐ __________
- ☐ __________
- ☐ __________
- ☐ __________
- ☐ __________
- ☐ __________
- ☐ __________
- ☐ __________
- ☐ __________

PACKING

MEDICATION

- First aid kit
- Prescribed medicine
- Prescription copy
- Allergy medicine
- Pain killers
- Motion sickness pills
- Altitude sickness pills
- Insect repellant
- Common cold
- Vitamins
- Antibiotics
- Contraception
- Laxatives
- Diarrhea medicine
- Eye drops
- Sleeping pills
- Sickness bags
- ____________
- ____________
- ____________
- ____________
- ____________
- ____________
- ____________
- ____________
- ____________
- ____________
- ____________

ELECTRONICS / TECH GEAR

- Phone
- Phone charger
- Laptop
- Laptop charger
- Watch
- Headphones
- Travel alarm clock
- Hair dryer
- E-reader
- E-reader charger
- iPad
- iPod
- Electric shaver
- Extra batteries
- Adapters
- Power banks
- Camera
- Camera charger
- Memory cards
- Selfie stick
- Tripod
- Travel iron
- Portable hotspot
- Portable luggage
  weighing scale
- ____________
- ____________
- ____________

PACKING

TOILETRIES

- ☐ Toothbrush
- ☐ Toothpaste
- ☐ Dental floss
- ☐ Mouth wash
- ☐ Hair brush
- ☐ Razors
- ☐ Soap
- ☐ Shampoo
- ☐ Conditioner
- ☐ Deodorant
- ☐ Perfume
- ☐ Nail clipper
- ☐ Nail filer
- ☐ Tweezers
- ☐ Ear buds
- ☐ Hand sanitizer
- ☐ Pocket tissues
- ☐ Toiletry kit
- ☐ Contact lens kit
- ☐ Face wash
- ☐ Toner
- ☐ Feminine hygiene products
- ☐ Moisturizer
- ☐ Sunblock
- ☐ Night creams
- ☐ Make up
- ☐ Talcum
- ☐ Oil

TOILETRIES

- ☐ Lip balm
- ☐ Lipsticks, lip gloss
- ☐ Hand cream
- ☐ Make up kit
- ☐ Make up remover
- ☐ Wipe pads
- ☐ Nail polish
- ☐ Nail polish remover
- ☐ Cotton pads
- ☐ Small travel mirror
- ☐ Toilet paper
- ☐ Small scissors
- ☐ Laundry detergent
- ☐ Shaving kit
- ☐ __________
- ☐ __________
- ☐ __________
- ☐ __________
- ☐ __________
- ☐ __________
- ☐ __________
- ☐ __________
- ☐ __________
- ☐ __________
- ☐ __________
- ☐ __________
- ☐ __________
- ☐ __________
- ☐ __________

PACKING

MONEY & DOCUMENTS

- ☐ Cash (local and foreign currency)
- ☐ Few US dollars
- ☐ Forex cards
- ☐ Credit cards
- ☐ Debit cards
- ☐ Travelers checks
- ☐ Emergency money
- ☐ Passport
- ☐ Visa
- ☐ Airline tickets
- ☐ Identification cards
- ☐ Boarding pass
- ☐ Copies of documents
- ☐ Driving license
- ☐ Hotel reservation document
- ☐ Insurance cards
- ☐ Passport size photos
- ☐ Travel itinerary
- ☐ __________
- ☐ __________
- ☐ __________
- ☐ __________
- ☐ __________
- ☐ __________
- ☐ __________
- ☐ __________

MISCELLANEOUS

- ☐ Wallet
- ☐ Safety pins
- ☐ Keys
- ☐ Sewing kit
- ☐ Ziplock bags
- ☐ Laundry bag
- ☐ Backpack
- ☐ Handbag
- ☐ Purse
- ☐ Beach bag
- ☐ Snacks
- ☐ Sleeping mask
- ☐ Eye mask
- ☐ Ear plugs
- ☐ Travel pillow
- ☐ Personal diary/journal
- ☐ Pen
- ☐ Umbrella
- ☐ Water bottle
- ☐ Cards/other games
- ☐ Travel/language guide
- ☐ Maps
- ☐ Travel flashlight
- ☐ Tea/coffee sachets
- ☐ Duct tape
- ☐ An extra bag
- ☐ Yoga mat
- ☐ __________

MISCELLANEOUS

- [ ] ___________
- [ ] ___________
- [ ] ___________
- [ ] ___________
- [ ] ___________
- [ ] ___________
- [ ] ___________
- [ ] ___________
- [ ] ___________
- [ ] ___________
- [ ] ___________
- [ ] ___________
- [ ] ___________
- [ ] ___________
- [ ] ___________
- [ ] ___________
- [ ] ___________
- [ ] ___________
- [ ] ___________
- [ ] ___________
- [ ] ___________

MISCELLANEOUS

- [ ] ___________
- [ ] ___________
- [ ] ___________
- [ ] ___________
- [ ] ___________
- [ ] ___________
- [ ] ___________
- [ ] ___________
- [ ] ___________
- [ ] ___________
- [ ] ___________
- [ ] ___________
- [ ] ___________
- [ ] ___________
- [ ] ___________
- [ ] ___________
- [ ] ___________
- [ ] ___________
- [ ] ___________
- [ ] ___________
- [ ] ___________

TRAVEL DETAILS AT A GLANCE

FLIGHT DETAILS

NAME OF DESTINATION			
DATE OF DEPARTURE			
NAME OF AIRPORT			
FLIGHT NUMBER			
TIME OF DEPARTURE			
TIME OF ARRIVAL			

ACCOMMODATION

NAME OF HOTEL/ OTHER			
LOCATION OF LODGING			
CHECK-IN TIME			
CHECK-OUT TIME			
ROOM NUMBER			

TRAVEL ITINERARY

Day	Things to do
1	
2	
3	
4	
5	
6	
7	
8	
9	
10	

TRAVEL ITINERARY

Day	Things to do
11	
12	
13	
14	
15	
16	
17	
18	
19	
20	

TRAVEL BUDGET AT A GLANCE

EXPENSES FOR	ESTIMATED	ACTUAL
TRANSPORTATION		
FLIGHTS		
TAXI/TRAIN/ BUS		
OTHER		
TOTAL		
ACCOMMODATION		
HOTEL/APARTMENT		
OTHER		
TOTAL		
MEALS		
BREAKFAST		
LUNCH		
TEA		
DINNER		
OTHER		
TOTAL		
DIVERTISSEMENTS		
SIGHTSEEING		
ACTIVITIES		
OTHER		
TOTAL		

TRAVEL BUDGET AT A GLANCE

EXPENSES FOR	ESTIMATED	ACTUAL
MISCELLANEOUS		
VISAS		
INSURANCE		
TRAVEL ESSENTIALS		
TOTAL		
TOTAL EXPENSES :		

MEMORY LANE...

Here you can write about some of your special moments during this trip, put your photos...

TRIP 3:

PLANNING

- ☐ Check out a few famous travel websites for things to see, do, and other basic information regarding your destination.
- ☐ Search for the best time to visit, based on weather (check weather at AccuWeather.com)
- ☐ Look for special holiday packages
- ☐ Watch YouTube videos
- ☐ Read travel guidebooks
- ☐ Make a list of places to visit, note their hours of opening, closing and the entrance fees
- ☐ Apply for visa (if applicable)
- ☐ Book flights
- ☐ Take insurance (travel/medical)
- ☐ Book accommodation
- ☐ Book internal transportation
- ☐ Get vaccinations
- ☐ If traveling internationally, convert your money to local currency (of destination)

- ☐ Activate international roaming or get an international sim card
- ☐ Prepare a day-to-day itinerary
- ☐ Make a list of all the places, restaurants that you want to visit
- ☐ Make a list of all the activities that you plan to do
- ☐ Prepare a list of stores /restaurants near your apartment (in case you are renting an apartment)
- ☐ Note important numbers such as ambulance, local police
- ☐ _______________
- ☐ _______________
- ☐ _______________
- ☐ _______________
- ☐ _______________
- ☐ _______________
- ☐ _______________
- ☐ _______________
- ☐ _______________
- ☐ _______________
- ☐ _______________
- ☐ _______________
- ☐ _______________

PLANNING

PLACES TO SEE

RESTAURANTS/ CAFES TO VISIT

PLANNING

ACTIVITIES TO DO

NOTES

PREPARATION

Essential Foreign Language Vocabulary

Word/Phrase in Foreign Language	Word/Phrase in English

Essential Foreign Language Vocabulary

Word/Phrase in Foreign Language	Word/Phrase in English

PREPARATION

THINGS TO DO

THINGS TO BUY

PREPARATION

THINGS TO DO ONE WEEK BEFORE...

- [ ] Personal grooming : skin/ nail/ hair care
- [ ] Go for a health check up
- [ ] Visit dentist
- [ ] Download a few travel apps
- [ ] Clean house
- [ ] Put valuables in a safe place
- [ ] Take care of your plants
- [ ] Take care of your pet
- [ ] Pay bills
- [ ] Buy medicines and other essentials
- [ ] Make copies of important travel documents
- [ ] Mail all important documents to yourself
- [ ] Buy and stock up on non-perishable food items
- [ ] Clean the refrigerator and get rid of perishables
- [ ] Web check-in (if available)
- [ ] Get car serviced (if traveling by car)
- [ ] Leave your itinerary with someone

- [ ] Confirm all your reservations
- [ ] Get packing done !
- [ ] __________________
- [ ] __________________
- [ ] __________________
- [ ] __________________
- [ ] __________________
- [ ] __________________
- [ ] __________________
- [ ] __________________
- [ ] __________________
- [ ] __________________
- [ ] __________________
- [ ] __________________
- [ ] __________________
- [ ] __________________
- [ ] __________________
- [ ] __________________
- [ ] __________________
- [ ] __________________
- [ ] __________________
- [ ] __________________
- [ ] __________________
- [ ] __________________
- [ ] __________________
- [ ] __________________

THINGS TO DO ONE DAY BEFORE...

- ☐ Charge all your electronic devices
- ☐ Switch off digital clocks
- ☐ Turn off appliances
- ☐ Turn off heating/cooling
- ☐ Turn off water
- ☐ Empty trash
- ☐ Hold newspapers
- ☐ Inform milkman
- ☐ Inform friends/neighbors
- ☐ Book a taxi for airport
- ☐ Weigh luggage
- ☐ Lock all windows, doors
- ☐ Cover all surfaces, devices, equipment
- ☐ Have a light homemade meal
- ☐ Sleep early to wake up fresh and all ready for your trip! :)
- ☐ __________________
- ☐ __________________
- ☐ __________________
- ☐ __________________
- ☐ __________________
- ☐ __________________
- ☐ __________________
- ☐ __________________

PACKING

CLOTHING & SHOES

- ☐ T-shirts
- ☐ Shirts
- ☐ Dresses
- ☐ Underwear
- ☐ Jeans/Pants
- ☐ Shorts
- ☐ Sweater
- ☐ Jacket
- ☐ Pajamas/ Sleepwear
- ☐ Swimsuit/ Swim Trunk
- ☐ Socks
- ☐ Stockings
- ☐ Skirts
- ☐ Raincoat
- ☐ Overcoat
- ☐ Joggers/Sweatpants
- ☐ Thermal Wear
- ☐ Walking Shoes
- ☐ Runners
- ☐ Flip Flops/ Slippers
- ☐ Heels
- ☐ Sandals
- ☐ Boots
- ☐ Shoe Bag
- ☐ Shoe Horn
- ☐ __________
- ☐ __________

ACCESSORIES

- ☐ Glasses
- ☐ Ties
- ☐ Scarves
- ☐ Earrings
- ☐ Jewelry
- ☐ Hats
- ☐ Caps
- ☐ Shawls/Wraps
- ☐ Belts
- ☐ Money Belt
- ☐ Beachwear
- ☐ Sunglasses
- ☐ Glasses Case
- ☐ Gloves
- ☐ Towels
- ☐ Handkerchiefs
- ☐ Swimming Gear
- ☐ Hair Accessories
- ☐ __________
- ☐ __________
- ☐ __________
- ☐ __________
- ☐ __________
- ☐ __________
- ☐ __________
- ☐ __________
- ☐ __________
- ☐ __________

PACKING

MEDICATION

- First aid kit
- Prescribed medicine
- Prescription copy
- Allergy medicine
- Pain killers
- Motion sickness pills
- Altitude sickness pills
- Insect repellant
- Common cold
- Vitamins
- Antibiotics
- Contraception
- Laxatives
- Diarrhea medicine
- Eye drops
- Sleeping pills
- Sickness bags
- _______________
- _______________
- _______________
- _______________
- _______________
- _______________
- _______________
- _______________
- _______________
- _______________
- _______________

ELECTRONICS / TECH GEAR

- Phone
- Phone charger
- Laptop
- Laptop charger
- Watch
- Headphones
- Travel alarm clock
- Hair dryer
- E-reader
- E-reader charger
- iPad
- iPod
- Electric shaver
- Extra batteries
- Adapters
- Power banks
- Camera
- Camera charger
- Memory cards
- Selfie stick
- Tripod
- Travel iron
- Portable hotspot
- Portable luggage weighing scale
- _______________
- _______________
- _______________

PACKING

TOILETRIES

- Toothbrush
- Toothpaste
- Dental floss
- Mouth wash
- Hair brush
- Razors
- Soap
- Shampoo
- Conditioner
- Deodorant
- Perfume
- Nail clipper
- Nail filer
- Tweezers
- Ear buds
- Hand sanitizer
- Pocket tissues
- Toiletry kit
- Contact lens kit
- Face wash
- Toner
- Feminine hygiene products
- Moisturizer
- Sunblock
- Night creams
- Make up
- Talcum
- Oil

TOILETRIES

- Lip balm
- Lipsticks, lip gloss
- Hand cream
- Make up kit
- Make up remover
- Wipe pads
- Nail polish
- Nail polish remover
- Cotton pads
- Small travel mirror
- Toilet paper
- Small scissors
- Laundry detergent
- Shaving kit
- ___________
- ___________
- ___________
- ___________
- ___________
- ___________
- ___________
- ___________
- ___________
- ___________
- ___________
- ___________
- ___________
- ___________

PACKING

MONEY & DOCUMENTS

- ☐ Cash (local and foreign currency)
- ☐ Few US dollars
- ☐ Forex cards
- ☐ Credit cards
- ☐ Debit cards
- ☐ Travelers checks
- ☐ Emergency money
- ☐ Passport
- ☐ Visa
- ☐ Airline tickets
- ☐ Identification cards
- ☐ Boarding pass
- ☐ Copies of documents
- ☐ Driving license
- ☐ Hotel reservation document
- ☐ Insurance cards
- ☐ Passport size photos
- ☐ Travel itinerary
- ☐ _______________
- ☐ _______________
- ☐ _______________
- ☐ _______________
- ☐ _______________
- ☐ _______________
- ☐ _______________
- ☐ _______________

MISCELLANEOUS

- ☐ Wallet
- ☐ Safety pins
- ☐ Keys
- ☐ Sewing kit
- ☐ Ziplock bags
- ☐ Laundry bag
- ☐ Backpack
- ☐ Handbag
- ☐ Purse
- ☐ Beach bag
- ☐ Snacks
- ☐ Sleeping mask
- ☐ Eye mask
- ☐ Ear plugs
- ☐ Travel pillow
- ☐ Personal diary/journal
- ☐ Pen
- ☐ Umbrella
- ☐ Water bottle
- ☐ Cards/other games
- ☐ Travel/language guide
- ☐ Maps
- ☐ Travel flashlight
- ☐ Tea/coffee sachets
- ☐ Duct tape
- ☐ An extra bag
- ☐ Yoga mat
- ☐ _______________

PACKING

MISCELLANEOUS

MISCELLANEOUS

TRAVEL DETAILS AT A GLANCE

FLIGHT DETAILS

NAME OF DESTINATION			
DATE OF DEPARTURE			
NAME OF AIRPORT			
FLIGHT NUMBER			
TIME OF DEPARTURE			
TIME OF ARRIVAL			

ACCOMMODATION

NAME OF HOTEL/ OTHER			
LOCATION OF LODGING			
CHECK-IN TIME			
CHECK-OUT TIME			
ROOM NUMBER			

TRAVEL ITINERARY

Day	Things to do
1	
2	
3	
4	
5	
6	
7	
8	
9	
10	

TRAVEL ITINERARY

Day	Things to do
11	
12	
13	
14	
15	
16	
17	
18	
19	
20	

TRAVEL BUDGET AT A GLANCE

EXPENSES FOR	ESTIMATED	ACTUAL
TRANSPORTATION		
FLIGHTS		
TAXI/TRAIN/ BUS		
OTHER		
TOTAL		
ACCOMMODATION		
HOTEL/APARTMENT		
OTHER		
TOTAL		
MEALS		
BREAKFAST		
LUNCH		
TEA		
DINNER		
OTHER		
TOTAL		
DIVERTISSEMENTS		
SIGHTSEEING		
ACTIVITIES		
OTHER		
TOTAL		

TRAVEL BUDGET AT A GLANCE

EXPENSES FOR	ESTIMATED	ACTUAL
MISCELLANEOUS		
VISAS		
INSURANCE		
TRAVEL ESSENTIALS		
TOTAL		
TOTAL EXPENSES :		

MEMORY LANE...

*Here you can write about some of your special
moments during this trip, put your photos...*

TRIP 4:

PLANNING

- ☐ Check out a few famous travel websites for things to see, do, and other basic information regarding your destination.
- ☐ Search for the best time to visit, based on weather (check weather at AccuWeather.com)
- ☐ Look for special holiday packages
- ☐ Watch YouTube videos
- ☐ Read travel guidebooks
- ☐ Make a list of places to visit, note their hours of opening, closing and the entrance fees
- ☐ Apply for visa (if applicable)
- ☐ Book flights
- ☐ Take insurance (travel/ medical)
- ☐ Book accommodation
- ☐ Book internal transportation
- ☐ Get vaccinations
- ☐ If traveling internationally, convert your money to local currency (of destination)

- ☐ Activate international roaming or get an international sim card
- ☐ Prepare a day-to-day itinerary
- ☐ Make a list of all the places, restaurants that you want to visit
- ☐ Make a list of all the activities that you plan to do
- ☐ Prepare a list of stores /restaurants near your apartment (in case you are renting an apartment)
- ☐ Note important numbers such as ambulance, local police
- ☐ _______________
- ☐ _______________
- ☐ _______________
- ☐ _______________
- ☐ _______________
- ☐ _______________
- ☐ _______________
- ☐ _______________
- ☐ _______________
- ☐ _______________
- ☐ _______________
- ☐ _______________
- ☐ _______________

PLANNING

PLACES TO SEE

RESTAURANTS/ CAFES TO VISIT

PLANNING

ACTIVITIES TO DO

NOTES

Essential Foreign Language Vocabulary

Word/Phrase in Foreign Language	Word/Phrase in English

PREPARATION

Essential Foreign Language Vocabulary

Word/Phrase in Foreign Language	Word/Phrase in English

PREPARATION

THINGS TO DO

- [ ]
- [ ]
- [ ]
- [ ]
- [ ]
- [ ]
- [ ]
- [ ]
- [ ]
- [ ]
- [ ]
- [ ]
- [ ]
- [ ]
- [ ]
- [ ]
- [ ]
- [ ]
- [ ]
- [ ]
- [ ]
- [ ]
- [ ]
- [ ]

THINGS TO BUY

- [ ]
- [ ]
- [ ]
- [ ]
- [ ]
- [ ]
- [ ]
- [ ]
- [ ]
- [ ]
- [ ]
- [ ]
- [ ]
- [ ]
- [ ]
- [ ]
- [ ]
- [ ]
- [ ]
- [ ]
- [ ]
- [ ]
- [ ]
- [ ]

PREPARATION

THINGS TO DO ONE WEEK BEFORE...

- ❑ Personal grooming : skin/ nail/ hair care
- ❑ Go for a health check up
- ❑ Visit dentist
- ❑ Download a few travel apps
- ❑ Clean house
- ❑ Put valuables in a safe place
- ❑ Take care of your plants
- ❑ Take care of your pet
- ❑ Pay bills
- ❑ Buy medicines and other essentials
- ❑ Make copies of important travel documents
- ❑ Mail all important documents to yourself
- ❑ Buy and stock up on non-perishable food items
- ❑ Clean the refrigerator and get rid of perishables
- ❑ Web check-in (if available)
- ❑ Get car serviced (if traveling by car)
- ❑ Leave your itinerary with someone

- ❑ Confirm all your reservations
- ❑ Get packing done !
- ❑ _______________________
- ❑ _______________________
- ❑ _______________________
- ❑ _______________________
- ❑ _______________________
- ❑ _______________________
- ❑ _______________________
- ❑ _______________________
- ❑ _______________________
- ❑ _______________________
- ❑ _______________________
- ❑ _______________________
- ❑ _______________________
- ❑ _______________________
- ❑ _______________________
- ❑ _______________________
- ❑ _______________________
- ❑ _______________________
- ❑ _______________________
- ❑ _______________________
- ❑ _______________________
- ❑ _______________________
- ❑ _______________________
- ❑ _______________________

- ☐ Charge all your electronic devices
- ☐ Switch off digital clocks
- ☐ Turn off appliances
- ☐ Turn off heating/cooling
- ☐ Turn off water
- ☐ Empty trash
- ☐ Hold newspapers
- ☐ Inform milkman
- ☐ Inform friends/neighbors
- ☐ Book a taxi for airport
- ☐ Weigh luggage
- ☐ Lock all windows, doors
- ☐ Cover all surfaces, devices, equipment
- ☐ Have a light homemade meal
- ☐ Sleep early to wake up fresh and all ready for your trip! :)
- ☐ _______________
- ☐ _______________
- ☐ _______________
- ☐ _______________
- ☐ _______________
- ☐ _______________
- ☐ _______________
- ☐ _______________

PACKING

CLOTHING & SHOES

- ☐ T-shirts
- ☐ Shirts
- ☐ Dresses
- ☐ Underwear
- ☐ Jeans/Pants
- ☐ Shorts
- ☐ Sweater
- ☐ Jacket
- ☐ Pajamas/ Sleepwear
- ☐ Swimsuit/ Swim Trunk
- ☐ Socks
- ☐ Stockings
- ☐ Skirts
- ☐ Raincoat
- ☐ Overcoat
- ☐ Joggers/Sweatpants
- ☐ Thermal Wear
- ☐ Walking Shoes
- ☐ Runners
- ☐ Flip Flops/ Slippers
- ☐ Heels
- ☐ Sandals
- ☐ Boots
- ☐ Shoe Bag
- ☐ Shoe Horn
- ☐ __________
- ☐ __________

ACCESSORIES

- ☐ Glasses
- ☐ Ties
- ☐ Scarves
- ☐ Earrings
- ☐ Jewelry
- ☐ Hats
- ☐ Caps
- ☐ Shawls/Wraps
- ☐ Belts
- ☐ Money Belt
- ☐ Beachwear
- ☐ Sunglasses
- ☐ Glasses Case
- ☐ Gloves
- ☐ Towels
- ☐ Handkerchiefs
- ☐ Swimming Gear
- ☐ Hair Accessories
- ☐ __________
- ☐ __________
- ☐ __________
- ☐ __________
- ☐ __________
- ☐ __________
- ☐ __________
- ☐ __________
- ☐ __________

PACKING

MEDICATION

- ☐ First aid kit
- ☐ Prescribed medicine
- ☐ Prescription copy
- ☐ Allergy medicine
- ☐ Pain killers
- ☐ Motion sickness pills
- ☐ Altitude sickness pills
- ☐ Insect repellant
- ☐ Common cold
- ☐ Vitamins
- ☐ Antibiotics
- ☐ Contraception
- ☐ Laxatives
- ☐ Diarrhea medicine
- ☐ Eye drops
- ☐ Sleeping pills
- ☐ Sickness bags
- ☐ __________
- ☐ __________
- ☐ __________
- ☐ __________
- ☐ __________
- ☐ __________
- ☐ __________
- ☐ __________
- ☐ __________
- ☐ __________

ELECTRONICS / TECH GEAR

- ☐ Phone
- ☐ Phone charger
- ☐ Laptop
- ☐ Laptop charger
- ☐ Watch
- ☐ Headphones
- ☐ Travel alarm clock
- ☐ Hair dryer
- ☐ E-reader
- ☐ E-reader charger
- ☐ iPad
- ☐ iPod
- ☐ Electric shaver
- ☐ Extra batteries
- ☐ Adapters
- ☐ Power banks
- ☐ Camera
- ☐ Camera charger
- ☐ Memory cards
- ☐ Selfie stick
- ☐ Tripod
- ☐ Travel iron
- ☐ Portable hotspot
- ☐ Portable luggage weighing scale
- ☐ __________
- ☐ __________
- ☐ __________

PACKING

TOILETRIES

- ☐ Toothbrush
- ☐ Toothpaste
- ☐ Dental floss
- ☐ Mouth wash
- ☐ Hair brush
- ☐ Razors
- ☐ Soap
- ☐ Shampoo
- ☐ Conditioner
- ☐ Deodorant
- ☐ Perfume
- ☐ Nail clipper
- ☐ Nail filer
- ☐ Tweezers
- ☐ Ear buds
- ☐ Hand sanitizer
- ☐ Pocket tissues
- ☐ Toiletry kit
- ☐ Contact lens kit
- ☐ Face wash
- ☐ Toner
- ☐ Feminine hygiene products
- ☐ Moisturizer
- ☐ Sunblock
- ☐ Night creams
- ☐ Make up
- ☐ Talcum
- ☐ Oil

TOILETRIES

- ☐ Lip balm
- ☐ Lipsticks, lip gloss
- ☐ Hand cream
- ☐ Make up kit
- ☐ Make up remover
- ☐ Wipe pads
- ☐ Nail polish
- ☐ Nail polish remover
- ☐ Cotton pads
- ☐ Small travel mirror
- ☐ Toilet paper
- ☐ Small scissors
- ☐ Laundry detergent
- ☐ Shaving kit
- ☐ __________
- ☐ __________
- ☐ __________
- ☐ __________
- ☐ __________
- ☐ __________
- ☐ __________
- ☐ __________
- ☐ __________
- ☐ __________
- ☐ __________
- ☐ __________
- ☐ __________
- ☐ __________

PACKING

MONEY & DOCUMENTS

- ☐ Cash (local and foreign currency)
- ☐ Few US dollars
- ☐ Forex cards
- ☐ Credit cards
- ☐ Debit cards
- ☐ Travelers checks
- ☐ Emergency money
- ☐ Passport
- ☐ Visa
- ☐ Airline tickets
- ☐ Identification cards
- ☐ Boarding pass
- ☐ Copies of documents
- ☐ Driving license
- ☐ Hotel reservation document
- ☐ Insurance cards
- ☐ Passport size photos
- ☐ Travel itinerary
- ☐ __________
- ☐ __________
- ☐ __________
- ☐ __________
- ☐ __________
- ☐ __________
- ☐ __________

MISCELLANEOUS

- ☐ Wallet
- ☐ Safety pins
- ☐ Keys
- ☐ Sewing kit
- ☐ Ziplock bags
- ☐ Laundry bag
- ☐ Backpack
- ☐ Handbag
- ☐ Purse
- ☐ Beach bag
- ☐ Snacks
- ☐ Sleeping mask
- ☐ Eye mask
- ☐ Ear plugs
- ☐ Travel pillow
- ☐ Personal diary/journal
- ☐ Pen
- ☐ Umbrella
- ☐ Water bottle
- ☐ Cards/other games
- ☐ Travel/language guide
- ☐ Maps
- ☐ Travel flashlight
- ☐ Tea/coffee sachets
- ☐ Duct tape
- ☐ An extra bag
- ☐ Yoga mat
- ☐ __________

PACKING

MISCELLANEOUS

MISCELLANEOUS

TRAVEL DETAILS AT A GLANCE

FLIGHT DETAILS

NAME OF DESTINATION			
DATE OF DEPARTURE			
NAME OF AIRPORT			
FLIGHT NUMBER			
TIME OF DEPARTURE			
TIME OF ARRIVAL			

ACCOMMODATION

NAME OF HOTEL/ OTHER			
LOCATION OF LODGING			
CHECK-IN TIME			
CHECK-OUT TIME			
ROOM NUMBER			

TRAVEL ITINERARY

Day	Things to do
1	
2	
3	
4	
5	
6	
7	
8	
9	
10	

TRAVEL ITINERARY

Day	Things to do
11	
12	
13	
14	
15	
16	
17	
18	
19	
20	

TRAVEL BUDGET AT A GLANCE

EXPENSES FOR	ESTIMATED	ACTUAL
TRANSPORTATION		
FLIGHTS		
TAXI/TRAIN/ BUS		
OTHER		
TOTAL		
ACCOMMODATION		
HOTEL/APARTMENT		
OTHER		
TOTAL		
MEALS		
BREAKFAST		
LUNCH		
TEA		
DINNER		
OTHER		
TOTAL		
DIVERTISSEMENTS		
SIGHTSEEING		
ACTIVITIES		
OTHER		
TOTAL		

TRAVEL BUDGET AT A GLANCE

EXPENSES FOR	ESTIMATED	ACTUAL
MISCELLANEOUS		
VISAS		
INSURANCE		
TRAVEL ESSENTIALS		
TOTAL		
TOTAL EXPENSES :		

MEMORY LANE...

*Here you can write about some of your special
moments during this trip, put your photos...*

Useful Travel Apps/Websites

- Skyscanner
- Rome2Rio
- Omio (formerly 'GoEuro')
- Google translate
- Google maps
- Google trips
- Citymapper
- BlaBlaCar
- Flixbus
- 9292
- Azair
- Just eat
- Couchsurfing
- Booking
- Airbnb
- TripAdvisor
- Tripline
- Pack Point
- Money manager
- TransferWise

www.ingramcontent.com/pod-product-compliance
Lightning Source LLC
LaVergne TN
LVHW091617170726
843492LV00007B/2458